Attract More of What You Want and Less of What You Don't Want

Have you noticed that sometimes what you need just falls into place or comes to you from an out-of-the-blue telephone call? Or you bump into someone on the street you have been thinking about? Have you ever met the perfect client or life partner, just by fate or by being at the right place at the right time? These experiences are evidence that we attract what we think about into our lives. Do you know someone who finds themselves in bad relationships repeatedly, and who always complains that they keep attracting the same kind of relationship? The Law of Attraction is at work for them too. The Law of Attraction may be defined as follows: I attract to my life whatever I give my attention, energy and focus to — whether positive or negative. By reading this book you will come to understand why and how this happens.

There are several words or expressions that describe evidence of the Law of Attraction. If you have ever used any of these words or expressions, you are referring to the Law of Attraction. Here are just a few:

♦ *Out-of-the-blue* ♦ *Fell into place* ♦ *Serendipity* ♦ *Synchronicity*
♦ *Coincidence* ♦ *Luck* ♦ *Fate* ♦ *Meant to be* ♦ *Karma*

In this book you will learn why these experiences happen. More importantly, you will discover how you can use the Law of Attraction more deliberately. You will be able to attract more of what you want and less of what you don't want. As a result, you will have your ideal client, your ideal job, your ideal relationship, your ideal vacation, your ideal health, more money in your life, and all your heart desires.

My goal is to get you to understand that your thoughts will materialize into your reality. Exactly how you think about your life is what will show up for you. It's time to overcome the reflection in the mirror and release those self-sabotaging thoughts in your head. It does not matter how big, how small, or how intelligent you are; what matters are your thoughts. Change your thoughts and you change your life. It's time to become the visionary of your own success. Whether you rise or fall, it is your thoughts that decide your outcomes.

Begin to see yourself and your life as the miraculous expression of divinity that it is. Do not waste another precious moment concerned about what should have been; instead, believe what can be. You have unique gifts, talents, and abilities that only belong to you. You are magical! You are creative! You are divine!

LIFE IN FOCUS

Focus on the Good Things

DR. VALERIE DAVID

"Life is like photography. You need the negatives to develop."

— Unknown

Foreword

Through the lens of perspective, we are limited by our own personal view finder. Have you ever taken photos with a professional camera? The various lens options give us control over what the eye of the camera views and in what light it sees through. I am far from a professional photographer, but I have always found it interesting that with just a few changes in equipment a photo can look completely different than the previous, all in the exact same location.

The human viewpoint is often similar. Let's pretend you and I hike to the top of a majestic mountain. I think you see what I see, just because we are both looking with human eyes. This is not always true. Perhaps your preferred surroundings involve skyscrapers, the busyness of city life and noise, while the top of a mountain is an earthly heaven to me. This one difference in perspective gives you and I two completely different feelings, visions, and sense of accomplishment.

How we approach challenges depends on what lens we choose to look through. Our approach also influences the final outcome. It is unhealthy to pretend that our thoughts are always positive. This is an impossible expectation of ourselves and others. It is also physically and mentally unhealthy to suppress negative thoughts or feelings. Finding the positive focal point isn't about ignoring the negative but rather naturally, authentically training your brain to give more attention to the infinite positive possibilities, in spite of the negative.

Have you ever taken a photo on your phone and tapped the screen directing the camera to highlight and sharpen the subject while blurring the background? This is where the book, *Life in Focus*, will direct your thought process. We know the blurred background of a photo could be the mess of a person's living room filled with toddler toys and jumping dogs, but we do not allow our brains to care as much when we choose to spotlight the vase of gorgeous, bright purple lilies the photographer intentionally created as the focal point.

Dr. Valerie David has brilliantly compiled a guide to help you determine just where you want your focus to be. Her exercises on how to get there provide clear steps that are accessible, even to the ambitious and busy. This is a no excuses kind of text that you can continue to fall back on at each stage of growth.

Her dedication as a mother, friend, leader, and author goes beyond this book or media. If you are ever in the presence of Valerie you will instantly understand that she is authentic in her love for others. She is enthusiastic and devoted to inspiring those around her to stay the course of their goals and palpable joy.

Enjoy the following content as you ask yourself, "Where is my focus?"

~ Dr. Melissa Carver

Dedication

I have always been motivated and inspired by the writings of the late Dr. Wayne Dyer. It is with deep appreciation that I thank him for sharing his message of "you will see it when you believe it." Belief activates faith, faith reveals blessings. My life is fuller and richer because of his teachings and messages. I owe a heartfelt and much deserved thank-you to the tens of thousands of people who follow me on Facebook, Instagram, and Twitter. To my daughter, Brittany, and my family who have been there for me since the beginning — supporting me physically, emotionally, and spiritually…My love to you always.

Table of Contents

Introduction

Recently, my nephew said to me, "Auntie, why is life filled with so many negative circumstances? Why are people so despondent and prefer to talk about the negative? What has happened to the world?" I responded by saying, "It is as though we are sleepwalking through our own lives. Social media has become our source of truth. Reality television is now our new reality. As humans, we must go through the negatives before experiencing the positives. We are the ultimate choice makers and each day we choose to either create the lives we want, or have our lives dictated by the world around us."

We start our lives as innocent human beings, full of love, promise, and hope. We start out without any memories or experiences. We are simply beautiful beings with the potential to achieve greatness in our lives. We are trusting, open, and curious as we begin to learn the world around us from the ones that we have been gifted to be a part of our lives. Then comes the onset of harsh relationships, abuse, conflict, and all of life's painful experiences, and we wonder if life is safe for us. As a result, we adapt and adjust to fit into the world of giants that try to control every aspect of our existence. As a result, we develop into some of these negative portraits, even if it is not our desire or intention.

This book is an inspirational guide, based on the premise that we come into this world with unconditional love, security, and wellbeing, which is crucial to our mental health. As we grow older, this positive force becomes buried under layers and layers of defense mechanisms. Yet, we can never escape the idea that love is our birthright. The purpose of *Life in Focus* is to help us recover and redefine the beauty and love that is our birthright. God created us, and we deserve to develop into the angels that God intended us to be.

Healing involves being willing to look at the areas of our life that are painful, and then filling them with light and love. It involves peeling away the layers of what happened, understanding those hurts, letting go of the past, and finally moving on to a better place of light and love. It is founded on the premise that we have compassion for ourselves, as well as that we affirm our divine right to live as we want, unapologetically, and unbothered by the opinions of others on how we should live.

Regaining our divinity and self-esteem requires that we undergo a process, much like the process of film development before the digital age, and this process allows for healing. Healing is a journey that is personal for each of us but is necessary if we want to recover our self-worth.

According to Wikipedia, photographic processing transforms a latent image into a visible image. Healing in our life involves a similar process of transforming old, worn out and negative ways of thinking and behavior into beautiful, positive images of love and light. Every human journey to enlightenment occurs in three stages:

1. Separation from what holds us back,
2. An encounter with our higher power, and
3. A return to our life in a new and refreshing way.

Each stage will symbolize a change in our life and will honor the growth that we accept.

The journey to mental, spiritual, and emotional health takes time. It involves a staged growth period nestled with healing and love. Because of the pace of our lives, I have written this guide, *Life in Focus*, as a seed of wisdom that will germinate and grow within you as you go along your life's journey. Use it daily to obtain ideas, thoughts, and words of wisdom, which will help to guide you to your higher self.

Remember that a beautiful picture begins as a negative, that requires a process to transform it into an ideal. Let nature take its course and transform your life into something that you never imagined. Transformation is a gradual process, that if nurtured and cocooned with love, will reveal the divine god or goddess that God intended you to be. God ordained you to be great.

So, from distraction to discipline, darkness to light, past to future, you have the power at any moment to take your life where you want it to go.

A Negative mind will never give you a Positive life.

Distraction

If you are like most people around the world, you can realistically say that there are many things in modern life that compete for your attention. Many of these things keep us distracted and unfocused — everything from television to social media, to life in general. You may rarely find time to have moments of silence, to just reflect, to quiet the mind, to refill your cup, to simply just be. The key to peace is through thanksgiving, through praise, and most importantly through silence.

Distractions keep you from achieving your goals; they keep you on a path of destruction. Rather than follow the path we were meant to follow, unfortunately, we are too often distracted by things that move us in the wrong direction. Technology, online games, too much time on Facebook, unpleasant habits, addictions, stress, busyness, and other meaningless distractions lead us astray. Instead of following *the pure light* of perfection we allow bright and shiny artificial things to sabotage our journey. So, what about you? Are you following your priorities and pure light to the right destination, or are you allowing artificial distractions to lead you in the wrong direction? Are you following the path you were meant to follow or are you letting meaningless things keep you from being your best self? The great news is that unlike sea turtles, we can think, adapt, and change direction when we realize we are following the wrong path. We can tune out the distractions and focus on our priorities, which then allows *the pure light to* lead us to an ocean of possibilities and a great future!

Self-Knowledge

Your heart knows in silence the secrets of the days and the nights. – Kahlil Gibran

So many people today are not enjoying their lives because of the condition of their minds. They constantly dwell on negative, destructive, harmful thoughts. They do not realize it, but the root cause of many of their problems is simply the fact that their thought life is out of control.

More than ever, we must realize that our lives follow our thoughts. If you think negative thoughts, then you are going to live a negative life. If you think discouraging, hopeless thoughts, or even mediocre thoughts, then your life is going to go down that exact same path of hopelessness and mediocrity. That is why we must take captive every thought and renew our mind with Spirit daily.

The one thing that keeps us from achieving success is our dominant thinking. I challenge you to think about your dominant thoughts. Do not let self-defeating thoughts linger in your mind. Instead, speak God's promises over your life. Declare that you are fearfully and wonderfully made in the image of the divine. Take captive every thought and renew your mind daily to align with His great and awesome promises for your life!

The power of self-knowledge is the power to change your life and to change the way you think about who you are. You were meant for greatness. Stop settling and living a life of mediocrity, and start living your amazing, best life today.

Learn to let go and flow with Life

Letting go is the key to flowing with life and flowing with life is the key to letting go.

The miracle of transformation occurs each day. At any moment, your life can be exactly what you want, but you must begin where you are. When you fight and resist the way your life is, you create a state of fear and upset that destroys your ability to see things clearly. When there is no clarity, you destroy your ability to make good decisions. This destroys your effectiveness and as such, it makes your situation worse.

Letting go is an inner action that removes resistance, which in turn releases your fears and insecurities. The moment you let go, everything changes. With the fear and worry gone, you become creative and can solve any problem or discover solutions that you never imagined.

Fear is created by the avoidance and resistance of some future event. For example, after being hired into your dream job you make an error that you believe is going to lead to the termination of your job. You think about the error so incessantly that one day you make a fatal error, and as a result you do lose your job. The simple fact that you focused so much energy on losing your job caused you to constantly worry about making an error until it was brought into fruition. Focus your time and energy on what you want to happen instead of living with the fear that something negative will happen.

If fear is going to lose its power, you need to think about what you want to bring into your life. As Susan Jeffers, author of *Feel the Fear and Do It Anyway*, would say, "Feel the fear and do it anyway." Recognize that letting go is a state of mind, and it removes the fear and upset that otherwise might be crippling and debilitating.

The moment you become willing to lose your old self in exchange for your new self, is the moment your vision will shift and allow you to become the best version of you. Grant yourself permission to become your higher self — a self that can love again, that can grow again; a self that can achieve all your goals and dreams; a self that can radiate unconditional love to all you meet.

To make the process of letting go easier, there are two important steps that you can take. The first step is to trust. Trust that no matter what happens, you are going to be fine. When you have confidence and assurance that in the end you are going to be fine, the process of letting go becomes easier. You become detached from the outcome, and you trust that your higher self will allow the answers to come to you. You restore those instincts that you were born with, the instincts of trust and faith.

When you do not trust, life becomes difficult. You give into our fears; you worry, again, about things that will never happen. Trust is a choice. It is something you create. It is a declaration that everything will be just fine.

The second and most crucial step to letting go is to be willing to feel and face your emotions. Be willing, in this moment, to acknowledge their space in your life, to come to terms with the fact that they exist. Everything that happens to us can give way to a new level of love and joy in our lives. Every hurt, every shame, every disappointment can transform us and our lives into something miraculous.

I challenge you today to let go and let life happen.

Your struggles make you strong

Struggles, challenges, and challenging times offer you much more value than any other time in your life. You cannot grow without struggle. You cannot get STRONGER without resistance. Think about a time in your life that may have been trying but it also made you better. Be grateful for the struggles. They build character and strength.

As you go through struggles in life, never lose sight of the greatness that is in you. Spirit knows your worth; He sees your potential. You may not understand everything you are going through right now. But hold your head up high knowing that Spirit is in control, and that He has a great plan and purpose for your life. Your dreams may not have turned out exactly as you had hoped, but God's ways are better and higher than our ways. When everyone else rejects you; remember, God stands before you with His arms open wide. He always accepts you. He always confirms your value. God sees your two good moves! You are His prized possession. No matter what you go through in life, no matter how many disappointments you suffer, your value in God's eyes will always remain the same. You will always be the apple of His eye. He will never give up on you, so do not give up on yourself.

That struggle that was sent to defy you will be the same struggle that will define you. Stay focused on your ideals, dreams, and goals, then watch as your life unfolds into the greatness that it was meant to be.

Doubt

Doubt will stop you from achieving your goals. You are what and who you hink you are. Your thoughts are creating your reality in every single moment. You tend to do whatever you think that you can do. When you doubt that it can be done, you are creating the space for it not to happen. We are co-creators of our reality and when we allow doubt and fear to come in, we send choice and opportunity out the window.

When you go to sleep and dream, you realize that anything is possible. In your dreams you can fly, you can hold conversations with people who have long since left this world, you can move forward, you can find money and become rich, and you can marry the person of your dreams. In your dreams you have no doubts that you can do anything that you can imagine. What if your waking life had the same absence of doubt? Think of what would be possible for you.

Doubt is a dream killer. Say no to doubts, they are all inside your mind, and you can control your mind. When doubts come to the surface, send them away with positive thoughts and affirmations such as:

1. I am strong.
2. I am powerful.
3. I have greatness inside me.
4. I am a healer.
5. Life loves me back.

Take control of doubt before it takes control of you. Focus your mind on the positives; dismiss any feelings of doubt.

You are capable. You are worthy. You are deserving. You can do it. Have faith. Know that you can overcome any obstacle. Visualize yourself carrying out the goals you have set for your life and imagine what that feeling would be like for you. Make the experience real and you will see it manifest in your life.

Believe in yourself

It is important, when creating the life you want, to begin a practice of believing in yourself and your abilities. This is the time that you must exercise your faith, because to believe in yourself is not always an easy task. Do not be concerned or worried as to how things will happen because anxiety and worry can stop the flow between the conscious and subconscious mind. Your challenge is to just believe.

Become as a child. Children are natural believers until told otherwise by adults. To a child everything is possible. You must begin to use your creative mind as a child. Believe that what you desire is already a reality. In fact, in your imagination, believe that your desire has already entered the physical realm. Believe that what you want will become a reality. In this way, you send a complete picture of the event to your subconscious mind, for the process to begin.

I also recommend that while you are still new at the creation process, that you keep your thoughts to yourself. Everyone will not or cannot always see your vision and can sometimes create limitations on your life because of their unbelief or negative thinking. However, as your belief becomes stronger and you begin to manifest your destiny, you will be able to tell others of your desires. Never allow someone else's negativity to penetrate your vision for your life or view of self.

As you believe, so shall you become. Believe in you.

Law of Abundance

Have you ever thought about all the times you experienced an unpleasant situation? In other words, have your negative thoughts ever manifested into reality? You lost your job, you had no money, your mate left you, or you had a bad accident? You are the creator of the unpleasant as well as the pleasant situations that show up in your life. "But how is this possible?", you might say. "Why would I want to create unpleasant situations in my life?" The answer is the same, your thoughts create your reality.

Your unconscious mind houses all your fears, anxieties, and worries. When you place your attention on a fear, the fear becomes a reality. For example, if you fear you will not have enough money to pay your bills, then you will not have enough money to pay your bills.

You see, wherever you place your attention is what will manifest in your life. Knowing this, would it not be better to place your attention on the things that you want to happen? This is the universal Law of Attraction — for what you focus on becomes your reality; it will bring to you what you will it to bring. Training your thoughts takes much willpower as you are often forced to work through and in many cases go against, the ideologies you were taught, that have since followed you throughout life.

The law of abundance works hand in hand with the law of attraction. There is always an abundance of opportunities, and you create or attract them with your thoughts. I challenge you today to activate your faith and belief, and begin to envision abundance in the areas of your life where there is lack.

Personal Responsibility

To live a truly creative life, you must first acknowledge that you are the creator of your own destiny. You must realize that what happens in your life is a direct result of your thoughts. You must begin to accept responsibility for yourself. A lot of us are afraid of the idea that we have free will and can use it in any manner we wish. Many of us go through life complaining about the situation in our lives and we see them as out of our control. In this way, we deny responsibility for the events that occur in our lives.

There are no events or situations outside of your control. You have complete freedom to change the things that are happening in your life. Only you can choose to live a happy or satisfying life, and if you are telling yourself that you must wait even one minute before you can begin, you are deluding yourself.

When we pretend that we need something outside of ourselves for our continued happiness or peace of mind, we experience what I call "attachment." We attach part of our self-worth to an outside event, person, or thing. Then we try to control our feelings of self-worth by trying to control that person, event, or thing. It will never work.

Creativity is your birthright. You have the free will to choose the life and experiences that are right for you. But I give you this warning: if you don't use it, you will lose it. In other words, if you don't make your own decisions, someone will make them for you, leaving you to wonder why you are always a "victim".

It is up to you to create the life you want. Do not wait for permission from another to unfold the real you. God has already granted you that permission. Use it to make the best possible life for yourself. Remember, you are the creating force in your life. Your thoughts will create your outcomes so choose them wisely.

I challenge you this day to choose what works for you and to allow for your greatest life to evolve.

Mental Ability

Your mind is a highly specialized, finely tuned, creative instrument. Scientists have worked for years to duplicate the functions of the human brain using computers and artificial intelligence. Your mind can be programmed for more efficient ideas by using exercises that strengthen your abilities in the areas of concentration, relaxation, imagination, will, and memory. Just as physical exercises work to refine the body, mental exercises work to refine the mind.

Do these few exercises and watch your desires manifest into what you want them to be:

1. Write down the things you want to happen as if you already had them and were enjoying them in the now.
2. Read your list and imagine yourself having and enjoying everything on it. Do this at least three times a day.
3. Be intentional with your thinking. When a negative thought enters, immediately replace it with a positive thought.
4. As you begin to achieve the things on your list, replace them with other things you desire.
5. When your list begins to work for you, don't panic; know that it is a tool designed to assist you on the journey to your desired life.

Learning to use your creative mind is akin to increasing your mental capacity, and just like developing any other skill in your life, it will take practice, patience, and persistence. Results will come quickly once you begin to follow through on your commitment and harness the power of your mind. Your mind is the great equalizer. You will begin to harness and direct the process. Increasing your mental capacity gives you the power to achieve anything you want in your life.

All of life is connected

Have you ever wondered why it is so easy to talk to a stranger? You are sitting in the airport and the person next to you just starts talking and you converse as if you have known the individual for life. There is a connection, a spiritual bond between all human beings on this earth. We come from various places in the world, but we all share the same things — we all want to love, take care of our families, make a difference in the world, and leave a meaningful impact. We only say them in different languages.

Fortunately for me, I had the opportunity to live and work in a foreign country and so I learned, firsthand, that we are more alike than we are different. Language, culture, and religion are the great dividers. But there is a human spirit that connects us all and a language that we all understand — love.

We have shown up in human form to be effective in this life and to teach our children to make a difference in the lives that they will touch. We have the most important opportunity to be effective and leave our footprint on humanity. How we show up each day is how we show up for each other. Do you show up with a smile or frown on your face? Do you show up happy or sad? Do you show up inspired and energetic, or do you show up depressed and down? Our energy and our moods shape the kind of environment that will develop.

Be known as the person that uplifts, inspires, and encourages. Leave negative emotions and feelings checked at the door. You have the power to change someone's life and in turn, change your own life. We are more connected than we can imagine; we are a part of a divine order created before the existence of time.

Be the change you wish to see in the world.

Give it up to have it all

Albert Einstein said that there are only two ways to live your life: one as though nothing is a miracle, or the other as though everything is a miracle. You must be willing to give up who you are to become who you want to be. Give up the illusion that you can get something for nothing; it is impossible. Give up looking for ways to bend the rules; you will only cheat yourself. Give up looking for a windfall; you only get what you give. Taking the uncomplicated or easy way out only gets you out of touch with God, and out of touch with the reality of how things happen in our lives.

Take life one day at a time. First, take a deep breath, decide what you want, and then put all your energies toward making your dream a reality. Realize that your efforts and your creativity are what make you come alive. Seeking fulfillment through possessions are empty pursuits that will leave you desperate and alone. Put your efforts and energies into becoming who you want to be instead of wasting them on jealousy and empty wishes.

Give up the need to be right or to get ahead; instead focus on all the abundance that is around you and all that you can give away to others. Focus on who you already are, who you can become, and who you are destined to be. Think of the life you can create if you allow Spirit to help you. Feed your faith, and your doubts will starve to death. Walk in your divinity. You are divine.

Alter your life by altering your thoughts

You have been endowed with the tools necessary to attract all good into your life. You have the power to overcome any weakness or faults of character. No matter how often you may have failed in the past or how tenacious others may have been at destroying you, YOU can win. Spirit gives you the power to reach prosperity of position without infringing on anyone else. There are a multitude of opportunities for everyone in this world. Spirit gives you the freedom of soul, body, and environment.

If you do not know what you want or what it is that would truly make you happy or better yet, fulfilled, then stop and ask yourself. Get in a quiet place and seek the divine wisdom that is your birthright. You have this independence, given at birth, so that you can build your life in the way that you choose to live. Remember that we are born with a set of instructions to live our lives to the fullest. We are given the power to understand and become our highest self. We are gifted human beings — if only we can believe that that all of life begins by altering our state of mind. The time is always right to change your thoughts. When you change your thoughts, you will certainly change your life.

Old ways won't open new doors

God is omnipotent; we are made in His image and likeness and as such, have power and dominion over our lives. How do we exercise this power in our daily lives? Harmony and peace of mind are simply carried out through thought. Stop thinking about the difficulty and instead start thinking about God. Think about what you want instead of what you don't want. We often have thoughts such as, I hope it does not rain or I hope that the other team loses the game. These kinds of thoughts will surely bring to pass the things that you don't want to happen. Instead, focus on the things that you do want to happen. "I am having a wonderful day. I have everything I need." It could absolutely be as simple as that. Old thoughts, habits, and ways of being will continue to give you results that you don't want. To have the things you desire, you will have to be willing to change the way that you see and think about your life.

Be careful of low energy thoughts as they only return to you. Examples of low energy thoughts include hate, anger, shame, guilt, and fear.

Instead, focus on high energy thoughts that will push you toward your dreams and your destiny. High energy thoughts include love, harmony, kindness, peace, and joy.

The key to your happiness is quite simple, not always easy, but simple. You must want to turn the page of your story to read the good news of your life. There is no power in the universe more powerful than God. Place your trust in an unwavering God and allow your life to unfold into greatness.

Finding your perfect place

Always in a state of flux, our spiritual life must be supported — similar to a household, a diet, a bank account, or a garden. Putting your choices into action is the key to living life fully. In learning to master your thoughts and emotions, your likes, your addictions, your passions, and your desires, life becomes less of a struggle and more of an orchestrated dance.

And yet, living fully and finding your perfect place is more than all these things. Finding your place is about a connection to the world in an integral way, a belonging that is vital, consequential, and immensely pleasurable.

To find your perfect place, you must discover and recover the missing pieces of your life. As you fill holes, you become whole. You will realize that you are divine. You are not bad, sick, confused, alone, or crazy, as you may have been told.

The negative before finding your perfect place becomes much like the chemical process endured by a beautiful photo in the development process. Mysteriously, moment after moment, the negative develops into the exact image that you saw in your mind. In finding your perfect place, you must dive deep and feed the Spirit, the life principle and animating force within yourself, and reclaim who you showed up to be.

In connecting with the mystical part of your being, you tap into the very essence of who you are, your center, your core, your soul, thus experiencing yourself in a larger way. This Spiritual dimension of who you are will supply a solid anchor of love, value, and worth.

"Every day we are engaged in a miracle that we don't even recognize: a blue sky, white clouds, green leaves, the black inquisitive eyes of a child, or simply your own eyes. All is a miracle." – Thich Nhat Hanh

And finally, inhabit your body. Listen to it. Learn to trust it. It is the source of deep wisdom and allows you to find your perfect place in the universe. Whether it is to inspire, teach, dream, explore, or simply just to be there for your loved ones. Embrace the divine that is you. Take care of your soul and treat your body well. Resolve to be your own best friend. Your physical, mental, and spiritual wellbeing should always be your biggest investment.

Rise above your burdens

The most senseless burdens are those of our own making. We live for the moment and disregard the future consequences. For example, we eat too much, exercise too little, put all sorts of chemicals in our body and expect that our bodies will still perform at its best. We let things slip and we do not follow up. The shortcuts eventually lead to our demise.

Yet, what we get ourselves into, we have the power to get ourselves out of. There is always hope; there is always a way to rise above your burdens. The same passion and energy that you send out to the universe that causes despair in your life is the same energy that can be evoked to change your life in a new and better direction. There is always hope.

Life can be so much more. Taking the easy way out is no way to live. The effort, the commitment, the discipline — these are their own rewards. Before you realize it, your life has shifted from one of trying to fail, to one of massive success and rewards. There is no effortless way out because the effort is the fulfillment.

Right now, right in this moment, you have the power to rise above any self-imposed burdens or failures. To achieve wholeness, you must uncover and recover the facets you have long ignored, denied, and/or neglected. Healthy developments demand that you have the courage to look at the entire picture and reclaim the missing pieces. The reclaiming of these missing pieces may be the very thing that enriches your life. You may discover a skill that you let go of, or a love that you had long forgotten because you were afraid to live from within. It can be scary to explore the unknown or areas that we have ignored. Yet keeping those parts of our lives hidden or undiscovered drains our energy and creativity and is a loss of potential.

An effortless way to rise above your burdens and tap into new sources of energy is to simply reframe and reclaim your birthright. You may find that you have discovered unexpected treasures. While at the same time you may discover areas that you have outgrown, and that no longer serve you.

Abundance is your natural state

For many people, abundance and success are tied to their level of self-worth and value. You make a good living, you pay your bills, and you save money, so you feel successful and abundant. For me, success and abundance are not what you have or how much you earn; success and abundance are measured by your ability to have inner peace and serenity. If you have inner peace no matter what the circumstance or situation, you can remain calm, peaceful, and serene.

I know that many of you may be thinking, peace does not pay the bills. I used to think the same thing. Many years ago, it appeared that all I created in my life was lack. Everything that I earned disappeared in bills, fees, or payments. The more I earned the more I spent, I could not get ahead. Then it finally hit me — my thoughts and beliefs were creating my reality. I realized that I could not feel abundance but at the same time worry about abundance. We attract to ourselves what we believe. I had closed the door to abundance just by my thoughts of lack. I began with a simple affirmation that my thought, which is my key to life, opens all doors for me.

You see, up until then, I had been looking outside of myself for the source of my supply. It's not outside of you, it's within you. Everything you need to be happy, prosperous, and live abundantly is inside of you right now. God's kingdom is within you, and you are an heir to this kingdom. You must recognize the divine sufficiency and constancy in your life. There is no scarcity or lack, only abundance.

Moreover, it is important to love what you do. For years, I have read about and watched successful people, and the common theme in their lives is that they have a passion and enthusiasm for their work. They love what they do. When you love what you do, you don't work, you are passionate and therefore you enjoy your life's work. Listen to your heart and follow what makes you happy. What gets you up in the morning? What would you still do even if you made no money from doing it? Pay close attention to the answers you get and be willing to respond.

Spirit can only do for you that which it can do through you. Open the door and let the light shine through you. Become an open conduit for receiving all that is abundant. Prosperity and love are our birthrights. Share what you love and love what you do, for these are the final steps to achieving abundance and reaching your highest potential.

Become an Agent of Change

Every life has at its core a dream that quietly and unobtrusively asks to be fulfilled. Each of us has a dream. It is an important part of the original blessing of being in this world. We have come to fulfill our life purpose. No matter how far we may have ventured away from our real purpose we can still become an agent of change. If you wish to realize your purpose in life and become an agent of change, start by relaxing. Relaxation allows for an open, unbounded, creative space. In this openness you can celebrate, that is, apply yourself — exercising your talents within the healthy boundaries of your chosen field or profession — getting what you want, and not giving it all away, but sharing it wisely. Relaxing, opening, and celebrating are three simple steps to individual wellbeing.

Woven into the formula for individual well-being is a need for supporting the global community, bringing our human endeavors into alignment with a partnership model of reality. This means that everybody wins. Although based on self-interest, everyone's actions can contribute to the highest good of all concerned.

If you wish to support, restructure, and become an agent of change in genuinely new and liberating ways, you cannot do so just by the same old way of being. Instead, you must start closer to home — with yourself, your personal integrity, your own energy. In other words, you, yourself, must become a whole and healthy individual. You must think for yourself emotionally and physically and follow your purpose in life, focusing on your own wholehearted wellbeing. Letting it flow through your life and out to others, will eventually help manifest wholeness for others and allow you the opportunity to be an agent of change.

Just as the negatives in film development become a beautiful work of art, so can the negatives in your life develop you to become a real agent of change.

Your Consciousness Is the Key

Your consciousness is the ultimate key to whatever you wish to experience in life. The path to enhanced spirituality, more joy, and financial abundance always lead back to your state of mind. If you are lonely, it does not mean that there are not enough people to love. In fact, there are plenty of people to love and situations that allow us to have more love. Viewed in a spiritual perspective, the loneliness we experience can be traced back to a barrier in our consciousness which keeps people away instead of allowing them into our lives. Many of the great spiritual teachers have taught us that we are eternal spirits with a mortal body. We play a key role in creating the events and circumstances of our lives.

If you broadcast thoughts of struggle and misery into the world, you will constantly attract negative situations into your life. In *The Game of Life and How to Play It*, Florence Scovel Shinn taught that our words are loaded with creative power, and that we should carefully select only words that bless, heal, and prosper others and ourselves. You can attract any good thing for which you are willing to pay the price for daily, with consistent affirmation. Affirmation comes from the Latin word affirmer, which means to make firm. The way a thought is made firm is in our consciousness through repletion. An affirmation is like a seed planted in the creative soil of the mind, which eventually germinates into reality. Through consistent care and watering, a seedling will grow into an oak tree. The same process occurs when you constantly affirm a statement in your mind.

The key is to say your affirmations over and over until the words seep into your subconscious mind, which is called the space of human desire. Just as it is important to take in the proper foods to keep your body functioning well, it is also equally nourishing to fill your mind with the right kinds of thoughts. The same God that suspends the heavens and ignites the stars is within you at this moment. Speak the truth of God's love and allow your subconsciousness to be your guide.

Reach Within

What lies within you is greater than anything that is outside of you. Most of us spend our lives looking for external or outside approval. In the era of social media, we tend to default to the person with the most likes and we dream to be more like that person. However, at our core we are perfect human beings, made in the likeness and image of an awesome God — crafted with greatness, kindness, and love.

In our first few years of life, we are innocent human beings and are so confident. We have high self-esteem and do not look to be like others. It is not until we reach school age that we begin to compare and identify with those around us. We look at others and want to have their hair color, their skin tone, or the shape of their hips — completely forgetting that we were born in the likeness and image of a magnificent God, created to do amazing things in this life. What we wish to have and be in this life is exactly what wants us. To live victoriously we must reach within and reclaim that part of us that was once confident and lovable.

To move from fear to confidence requires a strategy to protect oneself, both physically and emotionally. You need to know how to keep others from harming you. Once you accept responsibility for your feelings and how others make you feel, you will develop skills for protecting yourself when under attack. You must keep put-downs, criticism, prejudice, and humiliation from damaging your sense of self-worth. Without these skills you may turn to food, drugs, sex, shopping, or any addictive behavior pattern.

When having a conversation with someone, always consider the source; understand that person's intentions. Give more importance to what you think and less to what they think, and finally, don't take everything so personal because much of what people say and do are more about them than it is about you. Moreover, reach back and sift through what people say because what they are saying may have some truth however, they may lack the sensitivity to communicate in a way that causes you to miss the message. Develop tough skin and agree to disagree if necessary.

Finally, like all other skills, these skills will take practice. You don't have to tolerate put-downs. Protect your self-esteem and create more positive energy. You owe it to yourself and to doing your part to make the world a better place.

Do you know that you are magical?

We have all gone through life saying certain things about ourselves, such as: I am shy, I am intelligent, I am quiet, I am clumsy, I am skinny, I am slow, etc. Now that we understand the power of words and of the mind, we must come to the realization that these statements were simply creating self-fulfilling prophecies.

Consequently, we can now remake ourselves into the image of God. I know that this may seem tough to some, and even impossible to others but it is possible. Believe it. We are supposed to have the same attributes as our creator. We have attributes in His likeness such that we are loving, all knowing, able to create what we choose, eternal, forgiving, and peaceful. The creator of heaven and earth is also divine, has the power to overcome any challenge, and is immune to criticisms. Since we are made in His image, this makes these same attributes available to us.

We all have the power to be whoever we choose to be. If you have gone through life saying, "I am patient," then you have affirmed yourself into being that way. In the same way, if you have been saying all your life, "I am impatient," that's probably where you are now. Words and thoughts have power. The power to change your life. Every morning when you wake up, you have a new day ahead of you, and you can be whatever or whoever you choose to be. You can re-create yourself each day, especially when you consciously choose to let go of old resentments, grudges, fears, and habits.

Begin each day by affirming, "I have the power to create my moments." Once you make your intent known to your subconscious by that affirmation, it will cooperate in helping you to create that reality. Make sure that you are affirming what you want and not what you don't want.

Say to yourself, "I choose to be me and every day I am re-discovering who that is, without the condition of rules." Some people fear change, yet we are changing every single moment. You are not the same person that you were yesterday. Each day, each experience, takes us closer to our true nature and divinity.

Remember, there is no set definition of who you are. You are whoever or whatever you choose to be at that moment. Let your inner self and innermost desires lead you to who you are in every moment. You will not be disappointed. Let go of the definitions and labels given to you by society. Let go of the version of you shaped by family and friends that don't align with the greatness that is in you. Say to yourself in every moment, "I am so much more than anyone can imagine."

No choice is right or wrong; they are all simply experiences waiting to be unfolded. Live in the moment and make your choices accordingly. Live happily with who you are and make peace with your life. You are an amazing wonder of this universe just like the seven wonders of the world. You are indeed the eighth wonder.

What's holding you back?

By letting it go it all gets done. The world is won by those who let go. — Lao Tzu

There are so many of us who hate the idea of being wrong; we want to always be right, even at the risk of ending great friendships and relationships. We cause a great deal of stress and pain for us and for those around us. Whenever we feel the urgency to jump in and right a wrong, we must ask ourselves the question, "would I rather be right, or would I rather be kind?" Give up your need to always be right.

Be willing to give up your need to always control every situation and those things that are happening around you. Whether they are loved ones, coworkers, or just strangers you meet on the street — just allow them to be. Allow everything and everyone to be just as they are, and you will see how much better that will make you feel. Give up the need for control.

Have the courage to give up on blame and self-defeating talk. How many people are hurting themselves because of their negative, polluted, and repetitive self-defeating thoughts. Don't believe everything your mind tells you. You are better than that.

Other people are not responsible for how you respond to the world, only you can be responsible. Stop giving your power away and start taking responsibility for your life. As you believe, so shall you become. Give up your limiting beliefs about what you can or cannot do, about what is possible or impossible for your life. From this moment on, you are no longer going to allow your limiting beliefs to keep you stuck and bound to a life of mediocrity.

Give up your need to constantly complain about the many things, people, situations, and events that make you unhappy. No one can make you unhappy without your permission; you have to allow it. It's not the situation that triggers those feelings in you, but how you choose to look at the situation. Never underestimate the power of positive thinking.

Give up your need to be critical of things around you such as people, events, or situations. We are all different, yet we are all the same. We all want to be happy. We all want to love and be loved. We all want to be understood.

Forget the need to impress others or make others like you. Life doesn't work that way. The moment you stop trying so hard to control situations and those around you is the moment the masks come off; you can then be perfectly whole and allow those around you to be perfectly whole. You will effortlessly draw people and situations into your life.

Keep in mind that fear is just an illusion, it does not exist, it is created by you. It's all in your mind. Work on fixing the inside and the outside will fall into place. Starve your fears and its death is assured.

Finally, give up your attachment to the results and allow the work to take place quietly. When we are attached to the outcome, we are always checking the progress. When we let go of the outcome, the progress reveals itself. You will finally get to a place where you will be able to understand all things without even trying.

Your trials and sorrows develop you

Whatever good or bad fortune comes your way, give it meaning and transform it into something of value. Trouble is the common denominator of living. It's the great equalizer of life. Personal growth is the process of responding positively to change. All growth means change and change always involves risks, stepping from the known to the unknown. Your growth depends on your activity, or lack thereof. It only comes through continuous effort and struggle. You'll have no development without effort. Remember that falling is an accident but staying down is a choice.

Life chips and pounds at you to bring out your possibilities. She will strip you of wealth, humble your pride, humiliate your ambition, let you down from the ladder of fame, and discipline you in a thousand diverse ways if she can develop a little character. Everything gives way to that.

Wealth is nothing. Position is nothing. Fame is nothing. However, who you become inside is everything. What happens to you is not as important as how you react to what happens, for our present troubles are small and won't last very long.

I've learned nothing happens by accident. God knows what He is doing. Every valley has a blessing, and every valley has a purpose. There's no point in getting upset and letting trials sour your life. God promises His people victory! One day, you will look back and see what He was up to. Everything that you are going through will one day reveal itself to a deeper meaning.

Move past your limits

Most of us grow up with several limiting beliefs. We are told so often that we can't achieve success, or that we can't do this or do that. Most of us are in the habit of looking at the world through the narrow, limited perspective of our own interests. Certainly, it is important to look out for one's interest, yet there's a big world out there with a lot of people in it.

You benefit immensely when you expand your horizons and fortify your own perspective with the diverse perspective of others. Look at the situations in which you find yourself not only from your point of view, but also through the lens of those with whom you interact.

For each person you meet, ask yourself this question, "What can I do to provide this person with something of real and substantive value?" The answer to that question will open your eyes to an entire world of possibilities and opportunities which may have previously been hidden from your view.

Going past your own narrow interests is the best strategy for serving the sincerest of those interests. Every person with whom you come in contact is an opportunity for you to provide real value and, by so doing, to add genuine value to your own life.

Have true joy

Any moment of true, unencumbered joy is worth more than pure gold.

Try to experience more moments of pure joy and regularly lose yourself in bliss. You will think more clearly, be more motivated, feel better and be healthier. Do nothing to learn, to look good on your resume or to please anyone else. Don't try to impress your friends, family, or followers on social media. Learn to love you — simply for the experience of being fully alive and letting yourself completely enjoy all that is you.

You may be saying, "Is that selfish?" No. When you have more joy in your own life, you have more to give to others. By experiencing joy, you let the true person inside come to life. And that person is overflowing with love, abundance, and creativity, that will immensely add to your life as well as the lives of those around you.

Let yourself be joyful, without guilt, without expectations, without attachments. You will feel the power of that joy in every part of your life. This is our greatest achievement — to have true joy, to unfold, to be who we are fully meant to be.

Our challenges make us strong

The greatest challenge of anxiety is to choose one thought over another. Choosing faith when your present reality gives you every reason to fear and doubt can make it feel impossible to see anything beyond what anxiety is telling you. Every thought brings about an effect in your life. We can choose to allow our challenges to make us strong or cause us to retreat in fear. You have immense power to choose one thought over another.

You gain strength, courage, and confidence through every experience in which you look fear square in the face. You can say to yourself, "Fear has no control over me. These dark places have come to make me strong."

You may not realize it, but it's in the dark places that you really grow. They are where your character is developed, where you learn to trust God and to persevere, and where your spiritual muscles are made strong. In the dark places you pray more, you draw closer to God, and you take time to get quiet and listen to what He's saying. In those dark places you reevaluate your priorities, you slow down and take time for family, and you get a new appreciation for what God has given you. He has prepared you, developed your patience, humility, strength, and trust.

When you go through enough dark places, you don't complain about life's little inconveniences. You don't get upset because you didn't get a parking spot. You don't lose your joy when you get stuck in traffic. You don't get offended when a coworker is rude to you. You've been through too much to let these things sour you. Your backbone has been made into steel.

We can all trust God when we're resting in the green pastures, and we can trust Him when we're beside the still waters— that's easy. But He is asking you to trust Him when you're in the dark valley. He hasn't left you. You may feel alone, abandoned, and mistreated, and think that life hasn't been fair, but God is still leading you. That dark place is a part of the plan to make you into who you were created to be. It may not be easy, you may not understand it, but faith is trusting in God when life doesn't make sense. Dare to believe that He's blessing you even in the dark places. Believe that what's meant for your harm is going to work to your advantage, now and always.

Emerge a work of art

We may wait days for a negative to become a photo or work of art. When you want to change your life, and emerge a work of art, the negative must go. You cannot have a negative mind and expect a positive life. When you go through trials and hardships you will emerge a different person. These trials are what develop us through the negative, and result in a positive life.

Sometimes it's hard to be patient with the timetable of life. We, too, may be tempted to find a bypass or a shortcut but there are no shortcuts. Growth and development for bumblebees, butterflies, and humans alike, have their own timetable. We can stimulate and enhance growth, but we cannot force it to happen. Greatness needs time and persistence.

When we see and study nature, we learn a great deal about the process of growth and development. Seeds may lie dormant for a long time until the sun shines, the rain falls, or a rock is moved out of the way. When conditions are right, they grow, blossom, and bear fruit. Much like photography, we too must go through a process of growth and development to reveal the fullness of our life.

How do we know when it is time to emerge? Well, just like the flowers, they are planted, watered, and emerge in their own time. They need the right soil, sunlight, and climate, and before you realize it, they emerge into the beauties that they are destined to be. We can undermine the process by injecting our hate, doubt, and disappointments to affect our growth. How many times have you tried to sabotage your growth and development by saying things like, "I am not good enough." We can convince ourselves that we will always be a certain way. We can cling to the habitual, insecure thoughts and behaviors that create fear, stress, and anxiety that hold us back. We can also anesthetize ourselves through denial, distraction, and drugs, where we create an environment that causes of to ignore the gift to live more fully.

On the other hand, when we feel the urgings, we can say "Yes!" to the invitation to emerge and develop. We can shed the past and march full speed ahead into our future knowing that the creator fully supports us.

It may take days, it may take months, or it make take a few years before you are ready to emerge. Move at your own pace but make sure that you move. Be aware that this transition period can be the hardest and most vulnerable period of your life. Be gentle with yourself. Stay focused and let no one discourage you about your journey.

Your long history of pain and disappointment has prepared you to emerge. With your mind, intuition, heart, and free will, you can do anything. You can transcend your old beliefs and habits and create the world you want for yourself. You can indeed achieve miracles. Your primary responsibility, your destiny, is to show up and be who you are.

Be genuine

In a world with an insatiable appetite for social media, it has become easy to hide behind an avatar. We can easily pretend who we would like to be; however, many of us are afraid to show who we really are. Life has allowed you to come into being to fulfill a divine purpose. So don't allow the world to force you to pretend to be something that you are not. You were created in the image of God to manifest your destiny.

You will never change your life until you change something you do daily. If you learn to be your genuine self, you have the power to unlock all you need to succeed in life. When you waste time and energy trying to be something that you are not, you waste precious time on the things that you could be doing to change your life for the better.

Being genuine requires understanding who you are at your core. You are a child of God, crafted and made in His image — made to do amazing things in this life and to create a future for the next generation. Be the same person in the light that you are in the dark.

Affirm to yourself: "I just want to be who I am. I want to be that person who is at peace, genuine and true, not fighting to fit in, or trying to mold myself into what is socially acceptable. I want to be weird, silly, and dorky, with all my bizarre quirks and be loved for that. And I want to be my genuine nice self, full of compassion and understanding and be appreciated for that person, and not be taken advantage of. And I want to never allow someone's love for me to replace or substitute the love I need to have for myself."

When you are genuine with who you are, others will naturally want to be a part of what you are a part of. You allow others to love those darker parts of themselves. Never trade in your authenticity for approval.

The Power of Passion

How big are you willing to be? The power with which you dance through this life is absolutely and completely within your own hands. Your mind has the power to access infinite wisdom and prosperity, and your body can produce extraordinary health, vitality, and strength. They will do this for you, but only if you are willing.

If you are not willing, you will get what the rest of the world gets — pain, anger, despair, setbacks, and bad breaks. So, decide today that you will use the power of your subconscious mind to help you achieve your passion.

Most people do not achieve their goals or desires because they don't believe that they deserve it. Why, because years and years of society and families telling us to go to college, get a safe job, retire with your company, have robbed us of seeking our passion, the reason that we are here in the first place. You were born with infinite power and passion. That stirring in your soul is pulling you towards your destiny. Stop listening to the voices outside of you and learn to trust the internal yearnings found deep within you.

Furthermore, we are afraid. Our power is like a huge and unnatural tool to us, a roaring sea, but we are accustomed to the waters of the lake. All that is needed is that we wake up to the sea that is within us. You must be willing to allow yourself to take responsibility for who you are and begin the process of change, give up the old for the new.

Best of all you will know you are living as you were meant to live, at your maximum potential. The work ahead will no longer seem intimidating but something you look forward to undertaking. You will once again connect with the ripple effect of your power. Whether you realize it or not, you are hard-wired for success. Reclaim your power and your passion.

Creating with your imagination and your will

Everything that exists in the physical world began as a thought. Take a good look at your physical surroundings. Everything from this book that you are reading, to the chair that you are sitting on began as a thought in someone's mind. Remember, thoughts are things.

To create something you want, all you need to do is imagine it and then begin the necessary process to bring it into the physical. For example, let's say you want a new car. Imagine exactly the kind of car that you want, the color, the make, the style, and the cost. Imagine yourself sitting in the driver's seat, driving down the road. Imagine the joy and satisfaction you get from driving your new car. Use all your senses to experience your new car in your imagination. Imagine it and it will be yours.

The next step is to use your will to bring your new car to you. What this means is making the decision to get whatever it is you want and then following through with the decision by going out to get it. Since you know exactly what you want, your subconscious mind will take you directly to what you are looking for. Imagine it. Create it.

As you think in your mind, so is your reality

The mind guides our footsteps as we progress along the pathway of life. Our minds are the wellspring of what is brought forth in our lives. Our thoughts constantly create our reality. As the plant springs from, and could not be without the seed, so every act of ours springs from the hidden seeds of thought and could not have appeared without them.

Your success, your failure, your influence, your whole life is carried within you as your dominant thoughts decide your destiny. When I moved from thinking that I could not achieve something to thinking that I could achieve anything that I put my mind to, was when the light came on for me. I began to allow my thoughts to be more controlled. For example, if I thought a negative thought, I would acknowledge the thought and then release that thought. Moreover, I would replace it with a positive thought.

We are the unequivocal makers of our fate, be what it may. Each moment you are sending forth positive or negative thoughts that will decide your day. There is power and magic in the ability to control one thought over another, and as such change your life.

Cultivate then, a pure and unselfish spirit, and combine this with faith, and you will evolve and obtain abounding health, enduring success, greatness, and power. If your present moments are not what you want them to be, remember that you can change this at any moment.

As within, it is so without.

Gratitude

Gratitude is the great multiplier of life. When we are grateful for everything that shows up in our lives, we attract more remarkable things. Gratitude is defined as a spirit of thankfulness. It is so easy to complain but if you could turn your complaints into grateful thoughts, you will find that you have more than you can imagine. The result will be inner peace and an abundance of joy.

There is an urge towards growth and expansion in our lives; life is always seeking to express itself. Your desire to give more of yourself — more love, more happiness, more peace — all begin with a grateful heart. Our desire should never be to take advantage of others, but to inspire and uplift others.

Anything in the world that contributes to your success and happiness should be a blessing to others because we are all connected. The more joy and blessings you give to others, the more that you will have for yourself. We are all a part of creation and as we begin a practice of gratefulness and humility, everything shows up as a miracle.

What are you grateful for today? Are you grateful for God's love, mercy, and kindness? Are you grateful for the sun that shines and brings about the new day?

Gratefulness is a powerful force in our lives. No matter what may be happening in the world around you, you can always find something to thank God for. Gratefulness and faith go hand in hand. When we are grateful, it shows that our faith is bigger than our fears.

Remember, faith pleases God; it causes Him to move on your behalf. Work to develop an attitude of constant gratitude and give thanks to God for His goodness. As you do, you'll experience His mercy and loving-kindness in greater ways and move forward into the blessing and victory He has prepared for you.

Give love away

Do not feel lonely, the entire universe is inside you. — Rumi

The world has forgotten the real meaning of the word love. Love has been so abused and crucified by man that very few people know what true love is. Just as oil is present in every part of the olive, so love permeates every part of creation. But to define love is exceedingly difficult, for the same reason that words cannot fully describe the flavor of an orange. You must taste the fruit to know its flavor; the same is true as it pertains to love.

All of you have experienced love in some form in your hearts; therefore, you know a little bit about what it is. But you have not understood how to develop love, how to purify and expand it into divine love.

A spark of this divine love exists in most hearts in the beginning of life, but is usually lost, because man does not know how to cultivate it. Think deeply about what I am telling you. The satisfaction of love is not in the feeling itself, but in the joy that the feeling brings. Love gives joy. We love because it gives us such an intoxicating happiness. So, love is not the ultimate; the ultimate is bliss. Give love away every opportunity that you can; it will produce true bliss.

Love gives without expecting anything in return. I never think of anyone in terms of what he can do for me. And I never profess love to someone because he has done something for me. If I didn't feel love, I wouldn't pretend to give it; and since I feel it, I give it.

Love cannot be had for the asking; it comes only as a gift from the heart of another. Be certain of your feelings before you say to anyone, "I love you." Once you give your love, it must be forever — not because you want to be near that person, but because you want perfection for that soul. To wish for perfection for a loved one, and to feel pure joy in thinking of that soul is divine love.

Create your Life's Vision Statement

Many organizations around the world have a vision statement that guides their way of being. It's an aspirational statement that describes what the organization hopes to accomplish. Each of us should create a vision statement for our own life. What would your vision statement be?

First, start with who you think you are and what goals you want to achieve. More importantly, include the things that you value. Things such as trust, accountability, loyalty, collaboration, and integrity should be included in your vision statement. Keep in mind that what you value most is what tends to show up in your life.

Your thoughts are creating your reality. Create a vision so large that you scare yourself. This is not the time to think small, this is the time to rise to the occasion of who you are meant to be. Think big because the universe is waiting to serve your every wish. Also, keep in mind that as you pursue your dreams, you are inspiring others to live theirs.

A vision statement is a guidance tool for living your best life.

Create your Life's Mission Statement

Do not spend another moment of your life not living on purpose. Let everyone know that you came into this world for a purpose. And that purpose is to find your purpose so that you may live your life to the fullest. But how do you find your purpose?

Finding one's purpose begins with being able to identify the things that excite you or make you come alive. Everyone you know is gifted in a particular way. Everyone has a gift, a talent. The very essence of our soul's mission is to discover that gift and present it to the world. The problem for many is that they lack belief in themselves and in their own unique "gift." Sometimes those gifts are deeply buried, covered up by socialization, training, the demands of life, disappointments, and poor choices.

Society and school encourage conformity, fitting in with family or groups. Overdependency on mechanical devices discourages application of the human ability to do and to create. The passiveness of watching television and playing computer games diminish the creative imagination. Extreme specialization in most jobs and professions create boring, often repetitive routines and tasks, putting us in a rut. Constant busyness and too much to-do creates strain and distraction, cultivating the belief that we don't have time for something as serious as analyzing the true meaning of our existence, our purpose, our reason for being.

But the soul grows and develops as it discovers meaning, experiences reason, and sets goals for living. Spiritual understanding and development involve finding your soul self, your individuality, and expressing this universal part of yourself within physical life. Discovering your mission in life is only half the work; you must also live out your mission daily.

Create your own reality

You create and attract the things you want; you also attract the things you don't want. You attract the people in your life, the stuff inside your home, and the money in your bank accounts through your thoughts and feelings. When your beliefs are limited, you attract a limited reality.

Maintaining a meager mindset will compromise your well-being. Otherwise, when you expand your mind with limitless possibilities, those obstacles begin to break down. Embrace believing that anything is possible, that the sky is the limit. In fact, you can break through any situation with your positive thoughts. Sadly, whenever you focus on the "lack of" you are creating a less-than reality. When you encounter negative thoughts, you must switch your focus on being abundant and happy and as such, you will enjoy a luxurious and glorious reality.

Negative and limiting belief systems are buried deep inside us. Changing the idea of old habits that defeat you at every turn is possible. Are you up for the challenge? Start by learning how to break the habit of attracting negatives.

Start with these three effortless steps to attracting all your desires.

Ask - You must know what you want. I mean, really know what you want. The universe can't deliver without first knowing what it is that you want to have manifested into your life.

Believe - You need to honestly believe that what you are asking for will become yours. Doubts need to be pushed away. The idea that failure is a possibility will mess up the delivery.

Receive - It is important that you become an active player in reaching your goals. When opportunity comes your way, you must not hesitate. Grab the brass ring when it appears.

Discipline

Give up your need to always be right.

There are so many of us hate the idea of being wrong, wanting to always be right, even if at the risk of ending great relationships or causing a great deal of stress and pain to ourselves or others. It's just not worth it. When you feel a need to jump in and fight over who is right or who is wrong, ask yourself this question, would I rather be right, or would I rather be kind?

Give up your need for control.

Be willing to give up your need to always control everything that happens to you and around you. Whether it is your loved ones, coworkers, or just strangers you meet on the street, allow them to be who they are.

Give up blame.

Give up your need to blame others for what you have or don't have, for what you feel or don't feel. Stop giving away your power and start taking responsibility for your life.

Give up your self-defeating talk.

How many people hurt themselves because of their negative, polluted, self-defeating mindset? Don't believe everything that your mind is telling you; you are better than your thoughts. Be careful of what you tell yourself.

Give up your limiting beliefs.

As you believe, so shall you become. Give up the belief that you can or cannot do something, about what is possible or impossible for you. Never allow beliefs to keep you stuck in the wrong places.

Give up complaining.

Give up your constant need to complain about those things, people, situations, and events that make you unhappy, sad, or depressed. No one can make you unhappy; no situation can make you sad or miserable unless you allow it to. It's never the situation that triggers those feelings in you, but how you choose to look at it. Never underestimate the power of positive thinking.

Forget criticism.

Give up your need to criticize things, events, or people that are different than you. We are all different, yet we are all the same. We all want to be happy. We all want to love and be loved, and we all want to be understood.

Give up your need to impress others.

Stop trying so hard to be something that you are not just to make others like you. It doesn't work this way. The moment you stop trying to be something that you're not, the moment you take off your mask, the moment you accept and embrace the real you, is the moment you will find that people will be effortlessly drawn to you.

Give up your resistance to change.

Change is constant. Change will help you move from one area to another. Change will help you make improvements in your life and in the lives of those around you. Follow your bliss, embrace change, and don't resist it.

Give up labels.

Stop labeling those things, people, or events that you don't understand as being weird or different and try opening your mind, one small step at a time. Remember that your mind only works when it is open.

Give up your fears.

Fear is an illusion, it does not exist, it is created by your mind. Remember that Franklin D. Roosevelt quote, "The only thing to fear is fear itself." What fears are holding you back?

Give up your excuses.

Leave excuses behind, send them packing. You no longer need them. A lot of times we limit ourselves because of the many excuses we use. Instead of growing and working on improving ourselves and our lives, we are overcome with feelings of self-pity. Excuses begone!

Give up the past.

Stop deluding yourself, the past is behind you. Be present in everything you do and enjoy your life. After all, life is a journey, not a destination. Have a sharp vision for your future, prepare yourself, but always be present in the now.

Give up attachment.

This is a concept that, for most of us, is so hard to grasp and I must tell you that it was for me too, but nothing is impossible. We get better and better with time and practice. The moment you detach yourself from all things, you detach yourself from fear. Fear is the greatest opponent to achieving success. Where there is love there can't be fear because perfect love eliminates all fear. When you give up attachment you become so peaceful, so tolerant, so kind, and so serene. You will get to a place where you will be able to understand all things without even trying — a state beyond peace.

Give up living up to other people's expectations.

Far too many people are living a life that is not theirs to live. In other words, they are living someone else's dream. They live their lives according to what their parents, their colleagues, their teachers, or their friends think is best for them. They ignore their own inner voice, the very calling on their lives. They are so busy pleasing everyone but themselves. They forget what makes them happy. Do you know what you want, what you need, what makes you happy? You have one life and one life only, so make the best of your life and live in the now. Never let other people's opinions distract you from your path. Stay the course!

Twelve Powers of Life

FAITH: The ability to say yes to letting good manifest in your life.

LOVE: The ability to know and feel your oneness with all creation.

STRENGTH: The eternal, enduring quality of who you are.

WISDOM: The ability to discern what decisions best reflect your true self.

POWER: The ability to act, do, and carry out good.

IMAGINATION: The ability to form innovative ideas.

UNDERSTANDING: The ability to see good within all experiences regardless of appearance.

WILL: Your ability to align your personal will with God's will, and then to let your powers manifest that good through you.

ORDER: Your ability to think and act from a centered place in your consciousness.

ENTHUSIASM: Your ability to be interested and passionate about life.

LETTING GO: Your ability to release anything that does not serve you.

LIFE: That which is given to you to manifest the truth and beauty of yourself and all that you were born to be.

Affirmations for overcoming your challenges

- ♣ My strength is greater than any struggle.
- ♣ I am fearless.
- ♣ I'm getting stronger every day.
- ♣ I can do this.
- ♣ I'm deserving of my dreams.
- ♣ I was not made to give up.
- ♣ Broken wings will not stop me.
- ♣ No one can make me feel inferior.
- ♣ I know my power.
- ♣ Challenges are just opportunities.
- ♣ I do not fear the fire — I am the fire.
- ♣ I choose what I become.
- ♣ I am good enough.
- ♣ I'm brave enough to climb any mountain.
- ♣ I have the power to change my story.
- ♣ I feel joy no matter my situation.
- ♣ I am a warrior.
- ♣ My failures are steppingstones.

Conclusion

Life in Focus is about transformation. All transformation begins with an intense, burning desire to be transformed. You have all heard the phrase, "Be ye transformed by the renewing of your mind." In other words, to be transformed, the entire basis of your thoughts must change.

The first step in the "renewing of the mind" is that your desire must be different before you can begin to change. Then, you must visualize and declare your future dream a present fact. You do this by assuming the feeling of your wish fulfilled. By desiring to be other than what you are, you can create an ideal of the person you want to be and assume that you are already that person. If this assumption is continued on until it becomes your dominant feeling, the attainment of your ideal is inevitable. The ideal you hope to achieve is always ready for manifestation, but unless you yourself offer it your full attention, it is incapable of fruition.

Therefore, your attitude should be one in which having desired to express a higher state, you alone accept the task of bringing forth this new and greater version of yourself. Just as the moth in his desire to know the flame is willing to destroy himself, so must you in becoming a new person be willing to die to your present self. You must be conscious of being healthy if good health is your desire. You must be conscious of being secure if you are to know what security is. Therefore, to become a new and greater version of yourself, you must assume that you are already what and who you want to be, and then live by faith in this assumption. This is what wholeness means, this is what life in focus means.

Final Prayer of Protection

The light of God surrounds me.

The love of God enfolds me.

The power of God protects me.

The presence of God watches over me.

Wherever I am, God is!

Do not look for a sanctuary in anyone except yourself. — Buddha

About the Author

Dr. Valerie David is the author of several inspirational books. She writes and teaches about a subject she knows very well — inspiration and motivation. Over the years, Dr. David has done a complete overhaul of her very own life. Faith handles the new level of success and fulfillment she enjoys as an author and motivational speaker.

Dr. David grew up in South Carolina, where she was one of eight children. She knew early in her life that she had a special gift that today allows her to motivate and inspire every person that she meets. Dr. David has spent a lifetime seeking the golden nugget of truth; that is, we create our own reality. Her belief is that you can create the life you want by simply changing your thoughts.

Dr. Valerie David is passionate, engaged, and committed to ensuring that each and every person with whom she comes into contact, achieves their greatness, or at least are made aware of the great potential that is within. Her goal is to spread positive messages to everyone with whom she comes into contact, and to make sure we live our most amazing life. She enjoys traveling the world as well as learning about people through their culture. She also enjoys spending time with her grandson, Ashton, and reading about all things positive. Dr. David hopes to be an inspiration, through her writing and through the sharing of her journey, to anyone who wants or needs change in their life.

Travelers

We are travelers on a cosmic journey — stardust, swirling and dancing in the eddies and whirlpools of infinity.

Life is eternal.

But the expressions of life are ephemeral, momentary, transient.

We have stopped for a moment to encounter each other, to meet, to love, to share.

This is a precious moment, but it is transient. It is a little parenthesis in eternity.

If we share caring, lightheartedness, and love, we will create abundance and joy

for each other. And then this moment will have been worthwhile.

Deepak Chopra – *The Seven Spiritual Laws of Success*

Made in the USA
Columbia, SC
12 April 2023